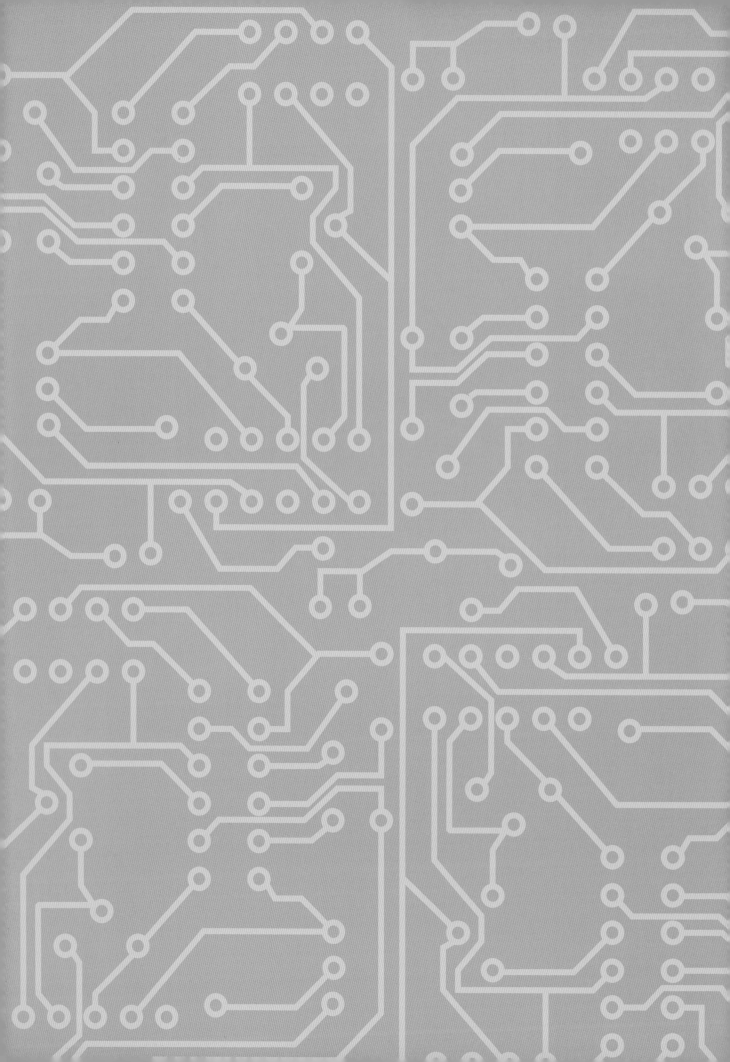

MARVEL
IRON MAN
BEGINNINGS

Based on the Marvel comic book series Iron Man
Adapted from Iron Man: Beginnings written by Jim McCann
Illustrated by Khoi Pham and Matt Milla

I'm billionaire Tony Stark. I'm sometimes known as the life of the party, but always known as the smartest man in the room.

I'm an inventor—not just because I inherited Stark Industries from my father but because I have to be.

© 2017 MARVEL

Published by Scholastic Australia in 2017.

Scholastic Australia Pty Limited
PO Box 579 Gosford NSW 2250
ABN 11 000 614 577
www.scholastic.com.au

Part of the Scholastic Group
Sydney • Auckland • New York • Toronto
• London • Mexico City • New Delhi
• Hong Kong • Buenos Aires • Puerto Rico

ISBN 978-1-74276-458-0

Printed in China by RR Donnelley.

Scholastic Australia's policy, in association with RR Donnelley, is to use papers that are renewable and made efficiently from wood grown in responsibly managed forests, so as to minimise its environmental footprint.

10 9 8 7 6 5 4 3 2   17 18 19 20 21 / 1

This glowing thing? It's in my chest not because it looks cool but because it keeps me alive.

I was captured by some pretty not-nice people after they used my father's company as their own weapons-supply store.

The explosion that knocked me out left me with tiny shards of metal inches from my heart. Still hurts. But I had a solution: I built the arc reactor—a machine that stays in my chest and keeps the metal at bay.

Why stop there? I'm the smartest guy in the room, remember? Well, in the cave, in this case. I used spare parts to build a metal suit that was also powered by the arc reactor. Then I put on the suit for a little payback.

It may have been clunky, but the suit worked for me on my first mission as

IRON MAN!

With a new purpose of saving lives as a Super Hero, I quickly built a better suit. A MUCH better suit . . .

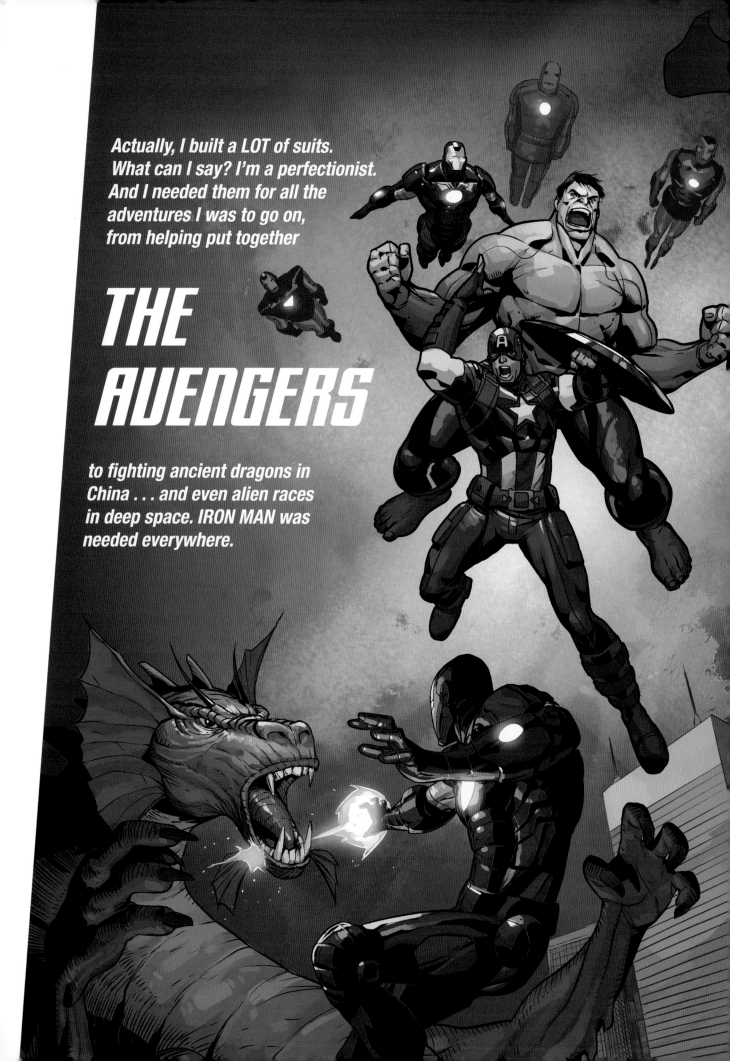

Actually, I built a LOT of suits. What can I say? I'm a perfectionist. And I needed them for all the adventures I was to go on, from helping put together

THE AVENGERS

to fighting ancient dragons in China . . . and even alien races in deep space. IRON MAN was needed everywhere.

But so was Tony. Running Stark Industries and making sure it leads every technological advancement —from phones to fans— can't be done alone. That's why I'm lucky to have

PEPPER POTTS

as my right hand.

I can't imagine what I'd do without her. She keeps Stark Industries running smoothly, especially when I need to keep Iron Man flying.

Although, she doesn't always like it when I take control, as you'll see . . .

'Everyone! Drop what you're doing,' said Tony. 'You have a new assignment.'

Pepper frowned. 'Excuse me? What about the wind turbines?'

'No, no, no. Tried that already,' he said. Tony showed Pepper and his engineers the plans for the new IRON MAN armour: COBALT—a remote-operated sidekick.

'This! This is what we're working on now . . .' But he was interrupted by a sudden burst of sirens.

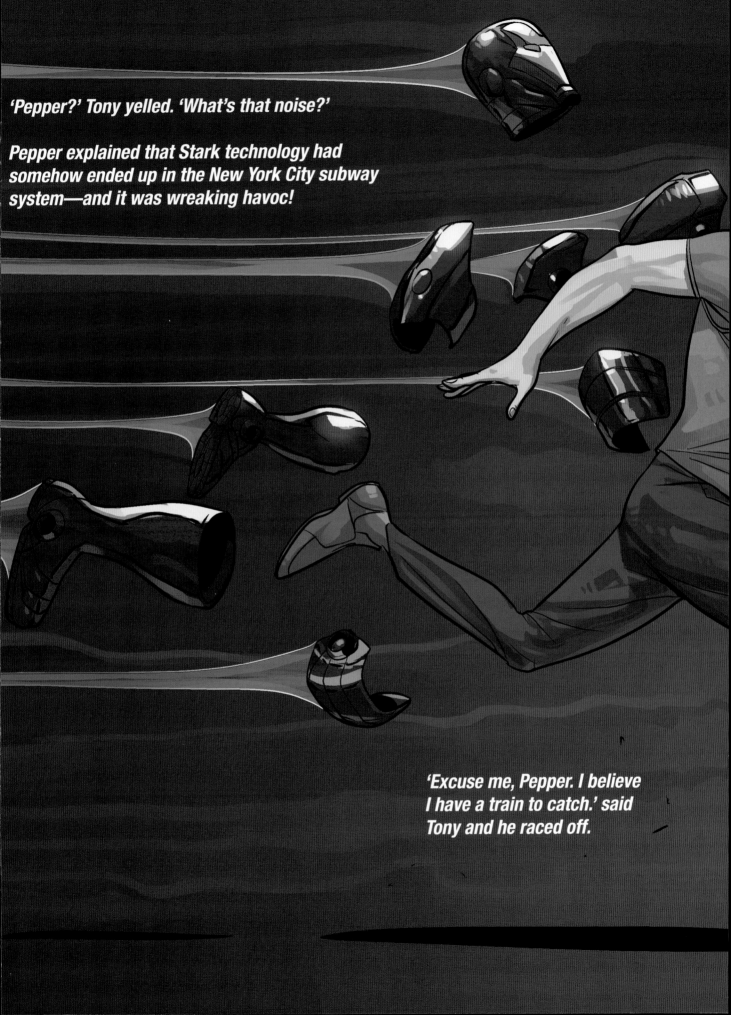

'Pepper?' Tony yelled. 'What's that noise?'

Pepper explained that Stark technology had somehow ended up in the New York City subway system—and it was wreaking havoc!

'Excuse me, Pepper. I believe I have a train to catch.' said Tony and he raced off.

In the heart of the city, people were running in fear! 'Help! There's a madman!' a woman cried.

Cyclone, the villainous wizard of wind, had escaped from the maximum-security prison, the Raft.

Cyclone seemed to have a suit upgraded with Stark technology. Now he was more powerful—and dangerous.

His wind tunnel lifted a train off the track and hurled it into the air.

Jet repulsors firing from his boots,
Iron Man used all his strength to
save the wind-whipped subway car
and its passengers . . .

Next, Iron Man turned to face Cyclone.

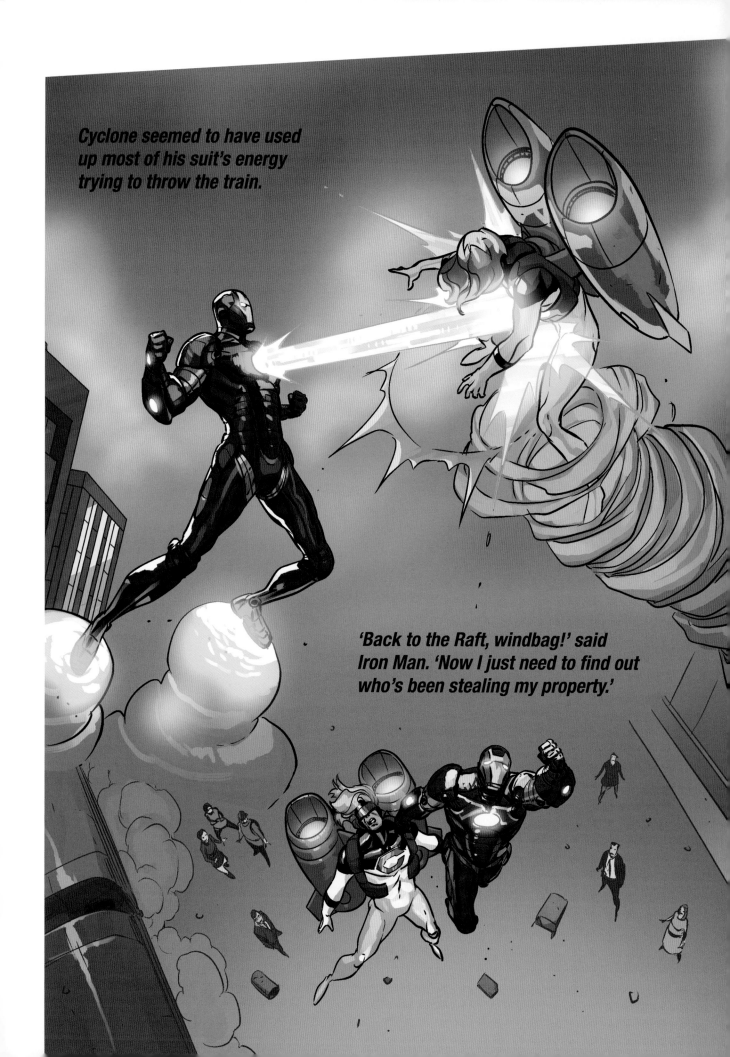

'We have a mole,' Pepper said and she handed Tony her tablet.

He immediately saw what she meant. 'Someone has hacked our system,' he said, 'and that's the garbage bin they've been rummaging through.'

'We've traced the source of the hack back to its origin: A.I.M.' Pepper confirmed.

Advanced Idea Mechanics was an evil rival of Stark's. A.I.M. had hacked into his system to steal discarded Stark Industries' ideas and design weapons for Super Villains.

Tony's brain was working in overdrive as an idea grew from a tiny particle to a fully ingenious plan . . . if he did say so himself.

Within a day, Iron Man was ready to test out his newest invention!

'Come on,' Iron Man said.
'Don't be shy.'

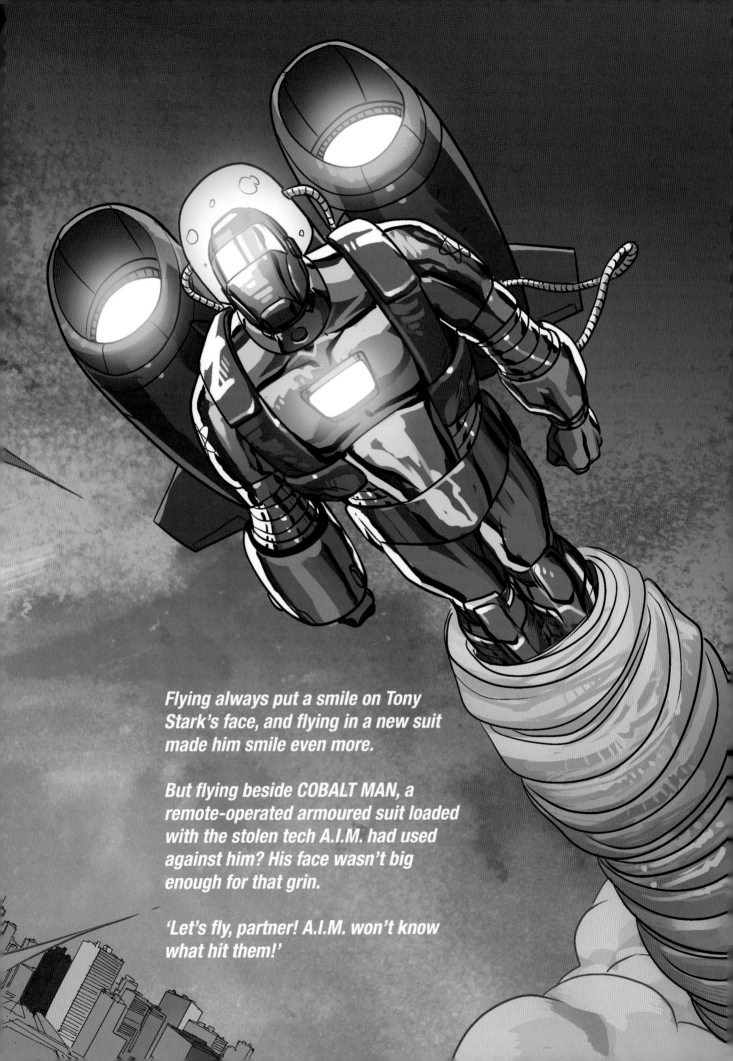

Flying always put a smile on Tony Stark's face, and flying in a new suit made him smile even more.

But flying beside COBALT MAN, a remote-operated armoured suit loaded with the stolen tech A.I.M. had used against him? His face wasn't big enough for that grin.

'Let's fly, partner! A.I.M. won't know what hit them!'

Between Iron Man and Cobalt Man, A.I.M. didn't really stand a chance.

'Didn't your parents teach you that stealing is bad?' Iron Man said to the commander, as he tied him up and set him down. 'I'm sure we can discuss how you broke past my firewalls when you're in your new home on the Raft. First, are all your troops accounted for?'

The commander nodded—and Iron Man gave Cobalt Man the final order.

'A.I.M. and fire, buddy. Give it everything!' Both suits unleashed their mighty energy weapons, destroying the base.

'Pepper, it's time to say goodbye to our new friend,' said Iron Man as he took full control of Cobalt Man's systems.

'Tony?' Pepper noticed Iron Man was sending Cobalt Man into a dive formation, directed at the remains of the base.

Tony didn't want any Stark technology to fall into the hands of his enemies. 'Unfortunately, that means losing my new toy,' he said. 'Maybe we'll meet again soon.'

The Raft. A prison for Super Villains of all types.

And the home of anyone who crosses Iron Man. 'Commander, I think visiting hours are next month. I'll swing by for that chat . . .

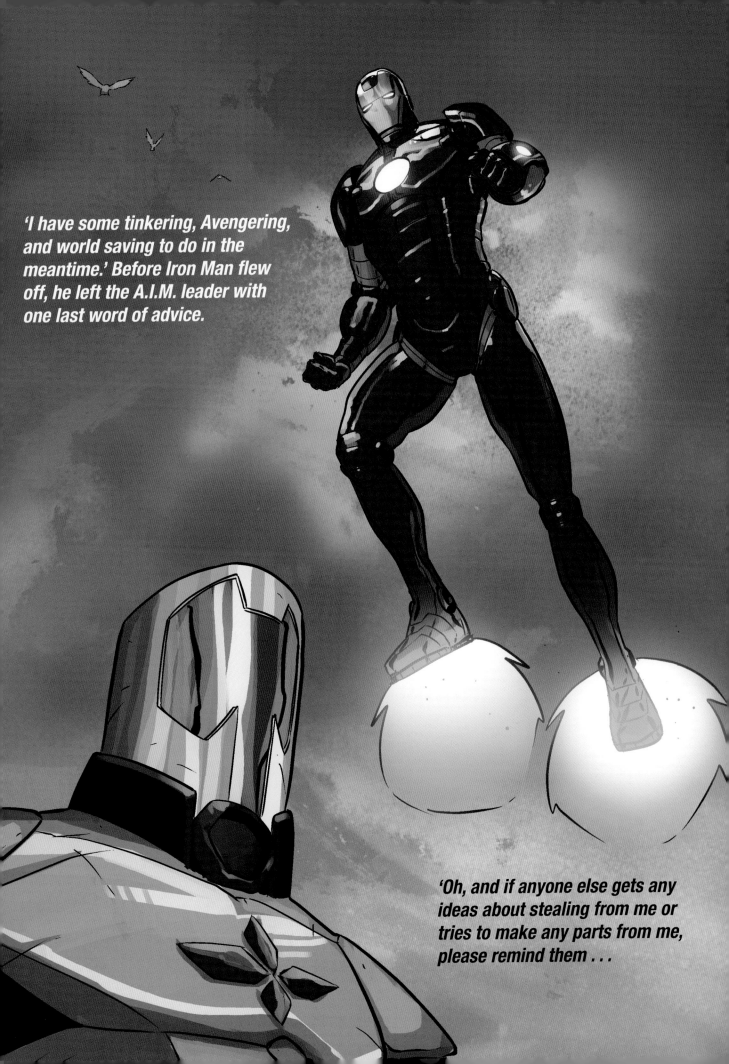

'I have some tinkering, Avengering, and world saving to do in the meantime.' Before Iron Man flew off, he left the A.I.M. leader with one last word of advice.

'Oh, and if anyone else gets any ideas about stealing from me or tries to make any parts from me, please remind them . . .

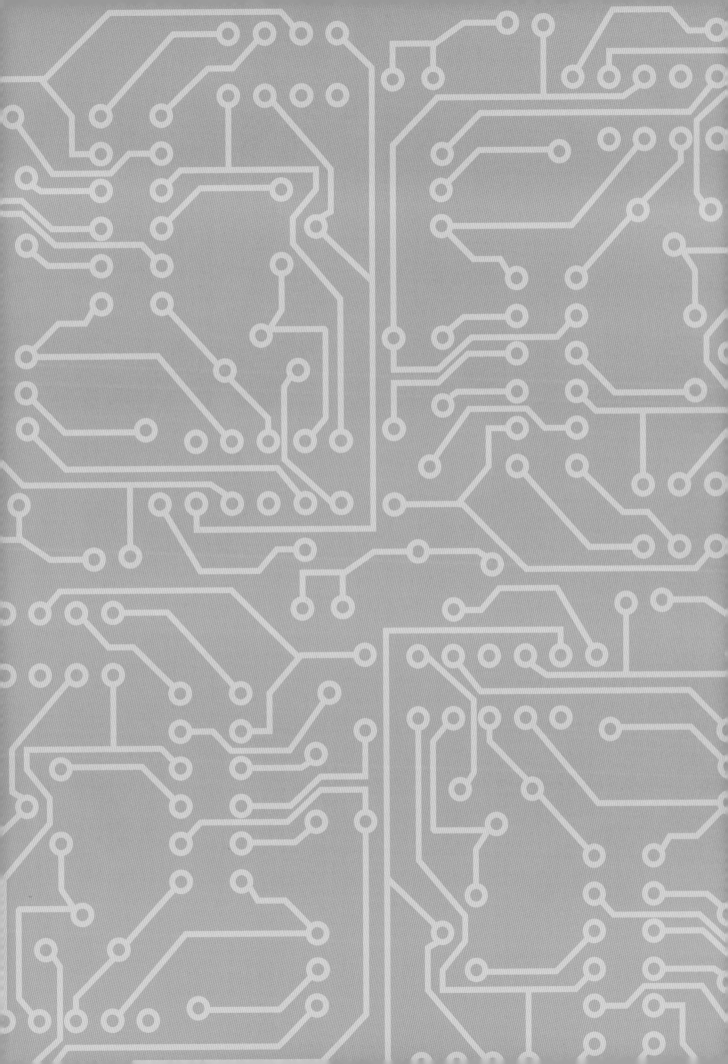